Car Mania

SPORTS CARS

Ryan James

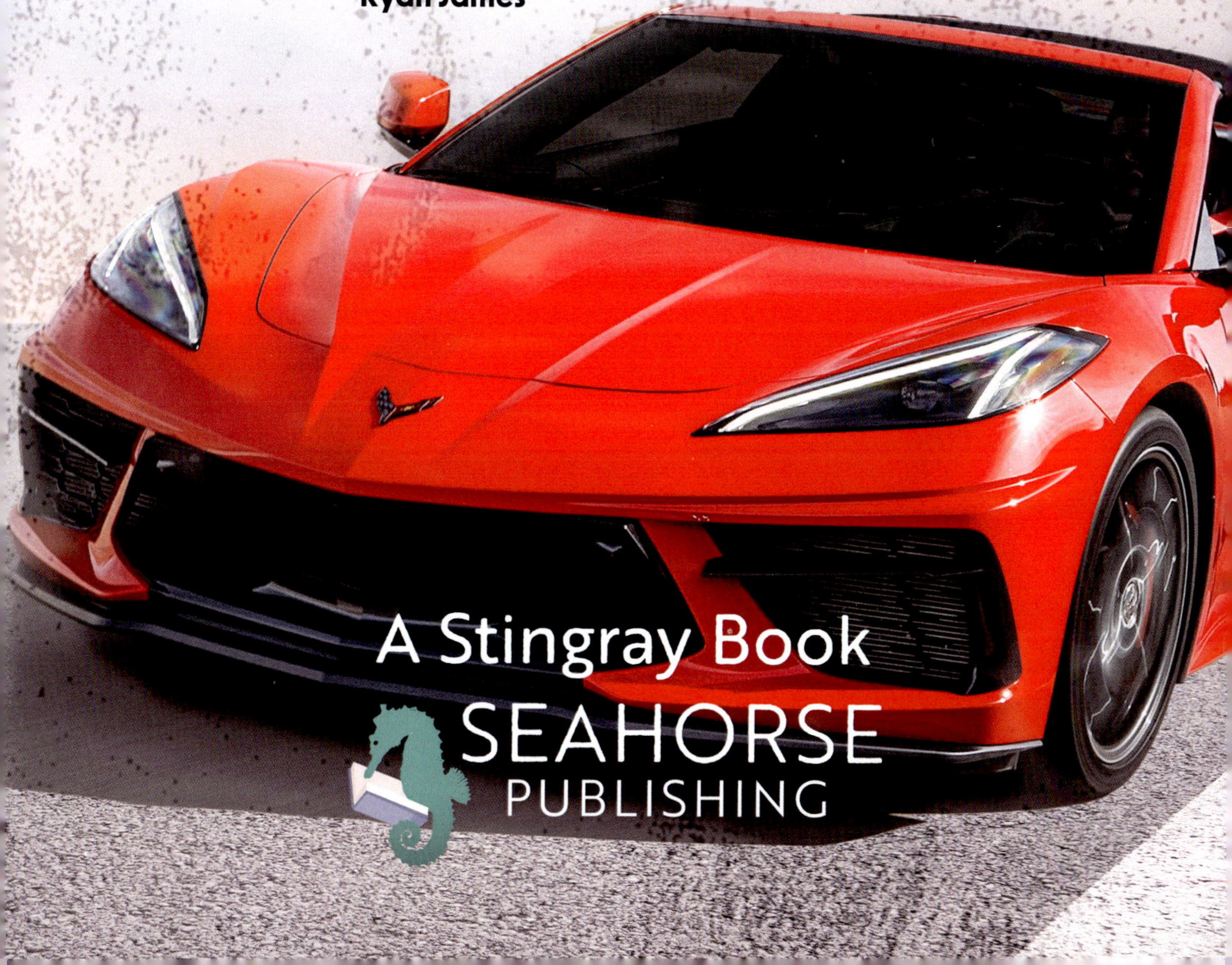

A Stingray Book

SEAHORSE PUBLISHING

Teaching Tips for Caregivers and Teachers:

This Hi-Lo book features high-interest subject matter that will appeal to all readers in intermediate and middle school grades. It may be enjoyed by students reading at or above grade level as well as by those who are looking for age-appropriate themes matched with a less challenging reading level. Hi-Lo books are ideal for ELL readers, too.

Each book appeals to a striving reader's age and maturity level. Opportunities are provided for students to read words they already know while encountering a limited number of new, high-interest vocabulary words. With these supports in place, students will read more fluent y while increasing reading comprehension. Use the following suggestions to help students grow as readers.

- Encourage the student to read independently at home.
- Encourage the student to practice reading aloud.
- Encourage activities that require reading.
- Establish a regular reading time.
- Have the student write questions about what they read.

Teaching Tips for Teachers:

Before Reading

- Ask, "What do I know about this topic?"
- Ask, "What do I want to learn about this topic?"

During Reading

- Ask, "What is the author trying to teach me?"
- Ask, "How is this like something I already know?"

After Reading

- Discuss how the text features (headings, index, etc.) help with understanding the topic.
- Ask, "What interesting or fun fact did you learn?"

TABLE OF CONTENTS

WHAT IS A SPORTS CAR?

Sports cars are more exciting to drive than other cars.

They are sleek and stylish.

They are fast and powerful.

They are designed to **outperform** other cars.

Most sports cars have only two seats. One is for the driver, and the other is for the passenger.

THE FIRST SPORTS CARS

In the 1920s, British **manufacturers** such as the Triumph Motor Company created the first sports cars.

Some car races at this time had cars go up unpaved hills.

Sports cars were the best at these types of races.

FUN FACTS

The Ferrari logo came from an Italian World War I fighter pilot named Count Francesco Baracca who painted a similar logo on his plane.

SPORTS CARS BECOME POPULAR

During World War II, American soldiers were sent to fight in Europe.

When they arrived, they saw sports cars and started driving them.

They liked how they looked and how simple they were to drive.

After the war, European companies such as Porsche started selling sports cars in the United States.

SPORTS CAR PARTS

Some sports cars have 12-cylinder **internal combustion engines**.

Other sports cars have electric or hybrid engines.

Many sports car engines get extra power from the addition of a **turbocharger**.

Wheels on sports cars are bigger than on other cars. Performance tires are designed to get better **traction** on the road.

FUN FACTS

The record-setting Koenigsegg Gemera can go from 0 to 60 miles (0 to 96.5 kilometers) per hour in only 1.9 seconds.

AMERICAN SPORTS CARS

Some sports cars are made in the United States.

Popular models are the Chevrolet Corvette, the Ford Mustang, and the Dodge Charger.

Powerful American-made sports cars can reach speeds of nearly 200 miles (322 kilometers) per hour.

But they may not be as **luxurious** as European sports cars.

EUROPEAN SPORTS CARS

Some sports cars are made in European countries such as Italy and Germany.

Models include the Lamborghini Aventador, the Audi R8, and the Ferrari 458 Italia.

Some of these cars go super-fast, but they are not allowed to be driven on regular roads.

They can cost one million dollars or more.

FUN FACTS

The 1962 Ferrari 250 GTO was the most expensive car sold at an auction. It sold for 48.4 million dollars in 2018.

SPORTS CARS IN ACTION

NASCAR (National Association for Stock Car Auto Racing) uses sports cars in their races.

The most common sports cars used in these races are the Ford Mustang and the Chevrolet Camaro.

These cars are built to be **aerodynamic** and to have good traction on sharp turns.

CAR SHOWS

Manufacturers show their new sports cars at car shows.

Car **enthusiasts** can look at a variety of vehicles all in one place. People can sit inside the cars or even drive them.

Drivers get to see the newest, fastest, most exciting sports cars.

TOP MODELS

AMERICAN

Chevrolet Corvette

First year in production: 1953

Average price: $67,000

Top speed: 194 mph (312 kph)

Chevrolet Camaro

First year in production: 1966

Average price: $30,000

Top speed: 202 mph (325 kph)

Ford Mustang

First year in production: 1964

Average price: $30,000

Top speed: 186 mph (299 kph)

EUROPEAN

Lamborghini Aventador

First year in production: 2011
Average price: $400,000
Top speed: 220 mph (355 kph)

Bugatti Chiron

First year in production: 2016
Average price: $3,000,000
Top speed: 305 mph (491 kph)

Ferrari 458 Italia

First year in production: 2009
Average price: $250,000
Top speed: 210 mph (340 kph)

GLOSSARY

aerodynamic (air-oh-dye-NAM-ik): having a shape that moves through air quickly and easily

enthusiasts (en-THOO-zee-ists): people who are passionate about a particular subject or activity

internal combustion engines (in-TUR-nuhl kuhm-BUS-chuhn EN-jins): machines that make cars move by burning gasoline in an enclosed space, producing hot gases that drive pistons

luxurious (lugh-ZHOOR-ee-uhs): comfortable, elegant, and expensive

manufacturers (man-yuh-FAK-chur-uhrs): companies that make products in a factory

outperform (out-pur-FORM): to work better than what is standard or ordinary

traction (TRAK-shuhn): the force that keeps a moving body from slipping on a surface, such as a moving tire on a road

turbocharger (TUR-boh-chahrj-uhr): a blower driven by exhaust gas turbines that is used to increase the power of an engine

INDEX

AFTER READING QUESTIONS

1. When did sports cars become popular in the United States?
2. How are sports cars different from other cars?
3. Why might a sports car be very expensive?
4. Why are sports cars used in NASCAR racing?
5. Where can drivers learn about new sports cars?

ABOUT THE AUTHOR

Ryan James lives in Western North Carolina with his dog Bailey. His favorite race to watch is the Daytona 500. His dream is to own a Lamborghini. When he's not writing books, you can find him backpacking through Pisgah Forest, North Carolina.

Written by: Ryan James
Design by: Kathy Walsh
Editor: Kim Thompson

Library of Congress PCN Data
Sports Cars / Ryan James
Car Mania
ISBN 978-1-63897-470-3 (hard cover)
ISBN 978-1-63897-585-4 (paperback)
ISBN 978-1-63897-700-1 (EPUB)
ISBN 978-1-63897-815-2 (eBook)
Library of Congress Control Number: 2022933100

Printed in the U.S.A./072025/CP20250717

Photographs/Shutterstock: Cover & Title Pg ©Chevrolet, ©Urse Major, ©Mooam, ©VoodooDot; Pg 3, 6, 8, 10, 12, 14, 16, 20, 22 ©Urse Major; Pg 7, 11, 15 ©Mooam; Pg 4 ©CParabolStudio; Pg 5 ©imtmphoto; Pg 6 ©FernandoV; Pg 7 ©Frank11; Pg 8 ©Massimo Campanari; Pg 9 ©Everyonephoto Studio; Pg 10 ©EA Photography; Pg 11 ©Erik Cox Photography; Pg 12 ©Ken Morris; Pg 13 ©Kevin Tichenor; Pg 14 ©Tom B Paye; Pg 15 ©Dan74; Pg 16 ©Grindstone Media Group; Pg 17 ©Art Konovalov; Pg 19 ©Chatchai Somwat; Pg 20 ©Clari Massimiliano, ©Steve Lagreca, ©Sarunyu L; Pg 21 ©PhatTai, ©supermodel, ©Roman.S-Photographer

Seahorse Publishing Company
www.seahorsepub.com

Published in the United States
Seahorse Publishing
PO Box 771325
Coral Springs, FL 33077

SEAHORSE PUBLISHING